PV: *'Style'*

Paul Vangelisti

ANOTHER YOU

*including 'Scapes', 'You', 'The
End of the Game' (a collaboration
with Giulia Niccolai & Adriano
Spatola), & 'Another You'*

The Red Hill Press
Los Angeles & Fairfax / 1980

Some of these poems have appeared in the following
publications: *Invisible City, Bachy, Critical Assembling,
City*, DOC(K)s (Marseilles), *The Fault, Tam-Tam*
(Mulino di Bazzano), *Zeta* (Udine).

Special thanks to Peter Goulds of LA Louver Gallery (Venice)
for loaning the works of Giulia Niccolai & Adriano Spatola
from 'The End of the Game'.

Cover: PV's 'Homage to William Xerra'

Publication funded in part by the NEA (a federal agency)

Distributed by SPD

The Red Hill Press
PO Box 2853
San Francisco, California 94126

Scapes

1

random as mountains of arid wind
above a clack
a high noon of
tin cans and chaparral
lowered Chevys and holler
hurry up
get back in the
clack clack across nowhere faster
than what had been bearably
random as

2

vitals say lung or brain tissue weighed for significant trace of
substances say lead or any foreign matter deposited say in the
air asymptomatic in children say chronic fatigue or occasional
loss of memory general defects in say maybe even

3

profit
or the memory of wealth
which is to say capital
or the memory of the body of the lord
which makes it November
shivering dusty nights
and almost anybody's ball game

4

crossed out vase of week old flowers nowhere the terror of a word
that begs terror getting this far and no farther than the nonsense of
windows growing thicker and no farther than 'thicker' so vague
and pervasive the windows brittle as calluses as windows after all
are terror after all the tickets have been sold

5

does it speak is it smile and play back your words often as you need
to talk out of both sides of the image you have of arriving home to
a replay of your smile out of both sides of the image you have of
your [words]

6

a flight up at least 50 years of polished wood he remembers some-
thing more than would he make it another place another time better
suited to ambulances or elephants or shoulders dancing upstairs to
the top of that voice yelling "get a job"

7

cockeyed hey don't make me laugh there are some men strapped
right to a tree look sport how bad can it be even if they say you
don't use English so good it's only been 12 years what do you
expect of her come on kid there's birds in the air wind in the
leaves what else do you need to die

8

she calls of what she calls
little but the dance of bright commerce
at the extraordinary edges of things

9

is this 'dance' this 'commerce' escape from that other commerce
not so brilliant in the eyes he heard her whisper look at his eyes
though he looks and sees nothing more precipitous than the room
at his back the moon outside swollen with hot wind he thinks what
he things fragile is no more so than on my knee her asking for the
old lyrics those rhymes to God she asks what God is is he Fifi

10

'moon outside' why come back to it is Fifi not enough swelling
with the nonsense of a vision of a daughter's voice is not enough
Fifi pregnant with never why these things these outside moon
desert wind these

11

fragile seems enough what it says though who on earth can imagine
what it says they're doing here must be yes or here must be the
same words the same place keep coming up in a snarl contrived to
simply get behind us cut away what they're doing here yes or no

12

or not saying yes or no about writing about the habit of everyday
more glass getting so you can't screw or look out at a hillside with-
out the definite feeling you've arrived here before the ambiguous
use of repetition maybe the glass or a conversation in the next room
seems unfortunately like the one interrupted last time he looked in
the mirror to say yes or

13

to exclude certain words to stare into dog's eyes Jack eyes dark
brown human name to stare excluding all that stares back because
he doesn't stare but the skyline does the Ford station wagon rolling
up the hill yes or no

14

unless it's the wind we're trying but what humor is there in that
midget planting his fingers on the big blonde's thigh with or with-
our cigar the midget that is maybe the blonde it doesn't matter to
the 12 women who telephone voracious protest of objects rendered
from the hubris of gnomes the largesse of full-hipped short-waisted
o, what has become of the morality of rain who will raise a voice
against the infamy of drainpipes yes or no

15

though even in purple the most prosaic drainpipe demands that we
need and what we get even if it's a glimpse through a dog's minute
we leave the words out to stare again at the roofs the skyline reflected
palm trees brilliant clouds reflected the rocking chair and French
windows on the TV screen growing dark in the west

16

if wrested is truly what words are certain of the 'mouthful of air'
each takes a menu glances across the freeway at a glass of ice water
where the voices the traffic sense the gaping mouth of what we
might momentarily stop for a [breath] of

17

tentative little indians true or false the spines of the palm or is it an
evergreen or do we navigate a sea of blood sharply do they bleed do
we come to begin again always at the same time strolling uphill
hand in hand shifting gears down to the memory of those shoes we
smiled in the library 12 years ago on home this is no place to think
of dying read the street signs it isn't raining yet

18

guilty as charged but how and to whom and for how long can she
remember the pain here a name there a name everywhere my father
pours he says don't go out in the rain they say it's snoring cats and
dogs straight from Chinese mushroom clouds they claim it per-
fectly safe as far as they know in the past it's always been the same
story forgive the pain but not the lies about the stains on the shirt
the eggflower the sweet and sour the paper-wrapped rain

19

from the bus window far as the eye can frame bar after bar of wheat
alfalfa oats occasional barn or horse resting dark against green
choruses of the eye receding to the presently cruel conclusions of
this [   ]

20

sketch might be the word left out as the bumps the peaches the
olive rows that are not green but bearably symmetric this time of
year 12 years ago

21

[t]eurat. tanna. la. rezus ame vachr lautn. aatiuth: arvasaapha. al. aal-
chuvaiseraturannuve. velthinas. e stla. afunas sleleth caru tezan. fusleri.
ri. athi. litiltalipilekatur. anuvecimima _ _ _ matesi. lesns teis rasnes. ipa
ama hen naper XII. araturanuve. velusi. velthinathuras. cras. pe ras ce-
mulm lescul zuci. en esci. epl tularu. siikanzich.

Yes

and left with talking and space and
an uncertain intensity
between maybe and someone and
deep flies in the blaze and gusty
February of outfielding
and outfields want time and space and syntax and a
propinquity for being specific about what nobody's
hands on the
foot on the
say hey can you see
who's on first and

*

she turns and says to him remember it well she is what her friends
called her she says 'next time we won't talk so much will we' until
he wants to take her [pale] neck between his fingers and not because
he was told to button it but that she used that terrifyingly first plural
as their friends called it in those days assuming he was looking
at her curly head pink hands too large eyes and writhing cigarette
and assuming he was even there to talk today remember it well
today is what their friends used to

*

hey can you says is seeing all you cannot empirically but in fact in
the eye yes in the eye all you can hope to touch husband to land
earth to sky high as the eye yes the eye can says you do and some
says you do what you don't really says you see the aye is a feel you
have for seeing what you says we're not I says we're not talking
about what you says really but seeing what you says you love when
you sees it until it dances up to you like the sun the size of a barn
and you can't get it out of your eyes no matter how bad you closes
them or shakes your head for wishing you had said it first

*

regardless of whether you is 34 or lefthanded or a preordained
factor in an already known movement or tendency away from
whether you is neither here nor there because you is what you's
expected to say yes or some to say no but always under the sun
almighty yes because it's only opinions that count among the no-
account and the best who are blessed in the land of was should and
forever will be yes and more yes from bumper to shining bumper
yes let us hear it from the brother in the back there with his head
tucked under his arm yes let him ride through our night swinging

those lantern righteous eyes because yes he is one of us sifting the
likely from the unlikely and yes though we says no and no though
we says yes it's always yes for the brother it's always yes for the sis-
ter it's always yes for the lover riding his headless ride through the
selfhood of this dark and yes this dark and yes this dark and

★

and when we walk
and when we stand
and when we smile
and when we sit
and when we talk
and when we tell
and when we sing
and when we reach
and when we stop
and when we go
and when we stumble
and when we look
and when we bend
and when we touch
and when we pause
and when we blink
and when we itch
and when we scratch
and when we hurry
and when we don't
and when we wait
and when we whistle
and when we stretch
and when we listen
and when we turn
and when we start
and when we should
and when we break
and when we run
and when we chase
and when we leap

★

and the mystery in fat is on the bone and the meanwhile in fact a
bastard to live since a question of a woman he danced until eight
years before he could dance with in short a habit of say a small
house and a play on her words he thought was dead however grave

he hears his own doubts turning over in the meantime of his sleep
of a steep wind and deep grass and her sea gray eyes of westerly
matter-of-fact afternoons they always together with the third the
small because in a very consequently thicket of silence as it burns
as always tangerine while they together he dreams although of his
own mouth

⋆

too steep to abandon to sight beyond the wheel of a purple loading
and reloading thumb and forefinger sighted over the windshield of
a grimy sleeping bang bang pair of precisely within a pinch of here
comes everybody looking like hell was yesterday and there's no
time left on the meter to brush teeth walk dog scratch ass to look in
the mirror for the crack in the glass in the dream sighted along a
very thin line of regret

⋆

and she says and he picks up the glass and she says and he closes his
eyes and she says and he stirs the soup and she says and he looks at
the spoon and she says and he leans back from the table and she says
and he gets to his feet and she says and he looks around for the salt
and pepper and she says and he moves back to the table and sits
down and she says and he drops some salt in his hand into the soup
and she says and he shakes some pepper into the bowl and she says
self-respect and he picks up the spoon and she says self-respect and
he puts down the spoon and she says and he gets to his feet takes
two steps to the refrigerator and she says and he opens the refrig-
erator and reaches for a beer and she says and he takes two steps
back to the table removes a glass from the cupboard sits down and
she says and he pours the beer and she says and he watches the head
rise in the glass and she says and he stands quickly eight steps to the
door twists the double-lock eight steps back and she says and he sits
down and she says and he looks at his glass of beer and she says and
he looks at his soup and she says and he picks up his spoon and
begins

⋆

or whatever possesses him to purple such waking of mirrors peek-
ing through medicine cabinets within an inch of making absolutely
no matter how many times he repeats the departure like hell was
yesterday and there's no meter left to time the brushing of teeth the
walk of a dog the scratch of an ass the length of a very thin

⋆

and begins to change pronouns midstream out the feet and ears as if
nodding off to pay the piper were not the piper but a spoon of a dif-
ferent color it however you wait it can't mean it isn't enough to
awake indefinitely and suppose as far as you can throw it consisting
it was all a long way to his own mouth

★

if edible simply is
what it's a question of
being as if
weren't they always
a lot of
knives and forks
on the job, brother?
so that free be anyone consummately not
to brush their dog's teeth
to vision their own mirrors miraculously
coming to walk themselves to sing to be
their own ass or not
monumentally in hell that is
in some thicket not yesterday but sometime
tomorrow and tomorrow to arrive thus
end this simply breath
of a damn song

★

boxcars belch the foggy tick
chopping each off the figures of
anyway he likes it
metaphor vision
don't mean a thing
if it ain't what he means
not what he means
but what he means when he wakes
and no one's there to listen

★

through light rain in Glendale he wakes
in Wrocław has to be Wrocław
when it's always been Glendale
far as Glendale means what he means
in Glendale
if he means no one there at all to

★

the test of the story seeing
that sure of Wrocław
gray like damp like
railroad sounds like
at least a [thought, heart,
etc] he saw Glendale waking
close as his [   ] on the floor
the torn [   ] in the corner
the ring of the disconnected
[   ] under the bed

*

ridding the ate of hearts or the inedible rereading of a goodly spoon
renegotiating the thought of a start a beginning an ending up syn-
onymous in a different week than the one run through the fingers
of downtown [   ] yes or

*

the rest of the story reading
footsteps cough through the wall
fingers buttocks
words scratched out
the salty roomful of sweet pain
and parentheses
jerked wide open
the eyes swallowed
of the final syllable whistles between delicious teeth

The End of the Game

The End of the Game was an exhibit & performance of
poetry involving Giulia Niccolai, Adriano Spatola & myself
at LA Louver Gallery (Venice, March 1–4, 1978) and at the
University of California (Berkeley, March 14–22, 1978). At
the left of each spread is Giulia's photo; at the upper right,
Adriano's image; while at the bottom right are my typed
texts. – PV

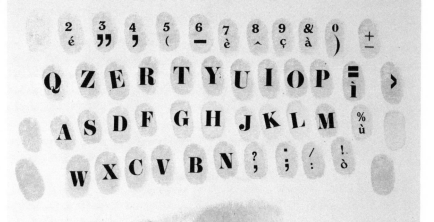

« From the First Key to Touch Typing »

```
tissue
'tis whom
and for how long
```

« *The Position of the Fingers on the Keyboard* »

```
above a clack
a high noon of
```

« Anagram »

```
Well, Well
Jose, can you see
through the wi(n)dow
```

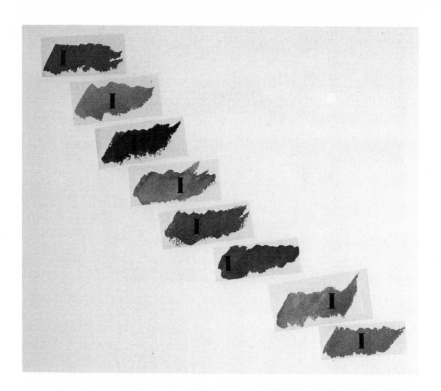

« *I* »

(   ) stares excluding all that
stares back because (   ) doesn't
stare back but the sky does

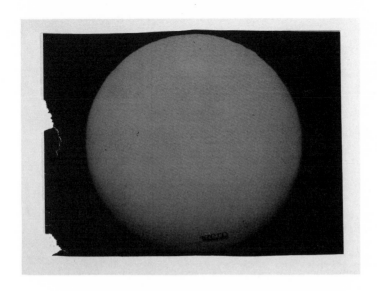

« Zero »

often as you have to talk back
out of both sides of the image
you have of your (words)

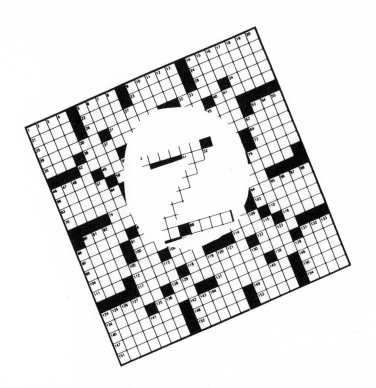

« *The Wizard of Oz* »

O the horns of plenty
O the morality of drainpipes

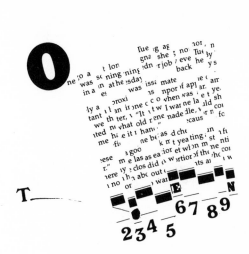

« *Ten* »

-tative little Indians
true or false

« Zen »

```
      a
-ttention
 even to the sun if it is out
 yes or no
```

Another You

You

the other one you rhyme
evening inflames
through a cracked window
faucet it hum like rain
woman sometimes
you can hardly speak to
that blind memory
in her eyes
who is there to love
but dream of your own mouth

An Elegance for Doda

*Carol Doda, queen of silicone and topless
dance; an imprint of her notorious glands
was donated to the city of San Francisco.*

even the sidewalk
discovers your breast
and if you were old
you are young
and if you were lost
you are found
buried tomorrow
in your snapshot of bones
own token of flesh
to the tips of your toes
the mountain crows
the sun shakes
even a tree knows
the moon speaks but once
and like sand flows
through the eyes of the dead
the clamor of snow
even a tree knows
the moon speaks but once
and like sand it snows
in the eyes of the dead
in the breast of the young

1970–1979

1970 Little is reproduced of his childhood

1971 As his lips are the body he imagines

1972 There's only the suitcase he isn't carrying with his left hand

1973 A bite that leaves no mark a bell without a tongue

1974 Door after door fly open with a twist of the hand

1975 A new life or so he begins to write to her

1976 Which is no one else's but hers who is not here

1977 Good night good night as in New York New York

1978 Or the old joke about the fastest draw in the West

1979 Well, well, Jose, can you see through the wi(n)dow

SIGNATURE *Paul Vangelisti*

DATE *3/19/79*

(t)eurat ame. te rezus hen

aisar athi. ri.

fusleri. la. arvasaapha

tularu teis esci.

al. velthinathuras. cras. pe ras.

epn lautn matesi.

clan. mach phersu epl suthina.

sech. capys velthinas.

ci. caru cassis. te vachr

tezan. lautni epl huth.

al. aalchuvaiseraturannuve.

en rasnes mi zilath.

tarchunies artile naper.

sa. etera. ci sleleth

tanna. al. araturannuve.

thu capys. aatiuth.

turan. zal fleres vipinas.

anuvecimima.

ϟⲦⳑΔ ⲒⴸⲖⲒ ⲘⲒ ⅎⱻⳑⴸϟⲒ ⲭΔⲭⴸ
st1a zuci. mi velusi cacu.

ⴸⴸⲘΔⵁ ΔⲘⅎ ⴸⴸⲒΔ
rumach. ame puia.

ⲦⴸⴸΔⲘⲘⲟϟ ⳑⴹϟⲭⴸⳑ ΔⴲⴸⲘΔϟ
turannos. lescul afunas.

ϟⲒⲒⲭΔⲘⲒⲒⵁ ⴸⲒ ϟΔ ⲒⴸΔ
siikanzich. ci sa. ipa

Δⴸⴹ ϟΔ ⲭⴸΔϟ ⲭΔⳑⴹ ⴲⅎⴸϟⴸ
aule. sa cras. caile phersu.

Ⲧⅎ ⲘΔⵁ ⲘⲒ ΔⲘΔ
te mach mi. ama.

Things To Come

This is dedicated to you for all the help

SEASIDE/ ~~for Robert Peters~~/ or seesaw or ~~maybe~~ the past tense ~~of candoadle~~

and understanding you've given me;

~~as the present~~/ of ice cream we ~~all~~ flesh the ~~dream~~ sinuous against a/

especially this last year. I've

neverending ~~sky~~/ though ~~it~~ shimmers alike the grace of ~~the~~ light ~~the fire~~

decided to move to a progressive and

~~and~~/ ~~the soft~~ the ~~bronze and pink~~ limits of desire ~~comprehensive~~ as/ the

friendly organization which has

~~incomprehensible~~ cries of children disappearing behind a/ ~~wave~~/ red and the

afforded me a tremendous opportunity

comfort and sun visors and towels and aluminum chairs/ ~~and red and purple~~/

for growth, with them as well as for

and their eyes at 20 as others at 45/ ~~lifting~~ the comfort of heliocopters

myself; which I'm extremely excited

~~bikinis and cabin cruisers~~/ detailed like cabin cruisers ~~bikinis and helio~~

about and know once you've seen it,

~~copters~~ against/ a ~~postcard sunset~~ everlasting at 20 as aluminum chairs at

I'm sure you'll share my enthusiasm.

45/ ~~as he stacks his beard to shave it off~~ or not to consider the/ ~~auto~~

I hope to see you soon at the Eli

swarming the sheet of paper ~~beach~~ i's ~~freeing the pen~~/ ~~the conception~~ of

Daresh Salon: 21390 Ventura Blvd.,

finishing ~~what was never begun~~ in the sense/ of ending what ~~started home~~

Woodland Hills, Tel. 982-7311.

~~phonous conjunctive conditionally green~~

Take care and until I see you again

Sincerely,

Self-Congratulatory on His 34th Birthday

happily to move among three or four things he said
against my preoccupation with syntax, prosody, the
common word, etc. etc., i.e., e.g., ' o you who
brought down Sodom and Gomorrah so you will bring
down the house and soul of _ _ _ _ _ ' (lapsus in ms.)
and not by the way but in fact I'm " ' which is to say
34 and not enough kind to this Italian typewriter and
keep first thing in the morning reading sentences in
the papers like 'In substance the district attorney
created a collage of . . .' becoming obvious I'm " '
tired of occasions or otherwise recalling only the
choruses of hundreds of tunes when there's a whole
transcendent world out there full of metaphors to
forget

14 *for Ania*

given repetition
and gypsies in such cruel fat
as demanding sombreros
who can bear parentheses
wet and big with the south
your south mine
anybody's dread
of the inelegance of the heart
the twitch of morning after
night before
even blank vaqueros
in the little I fiddle
as violins circle a page
of empty tables

Anaerobics or Else

Wait a minute, darling, is it you or
Isaac Newton who's been hanging around these
300 years to sink his teeth into a
truly deluxe leatherbound volume
on apples? What are you doing here if
you think I'm obtuse when it comes to molecules?
Maybe it's you, satin, who's queer for
researchers discreetly unlearning
all the rules about partridges and pears;
and this hex of yours, so uptight at any talk
of fine old-fashioned oral gardening.
Listen, sweetmeat, these ears are the only stairs
I got to heaven. Shut the light and conserve
the scientific method for the morning.

Madame O

of a young man
who approximately once
squeezed the letters DESPERATE
on the dark corner of a darker page
after chasing after a younger man
chasing after a chorus of streetcars
only to catch the fall invisible
the inner other city he pronounced
tender in continence of summer
feminine as buttons of lapsed milk
imagining how many you slay
with that fatal word you as in you
after imagining how many you slay
without that fatal word

Another You

and which about some of it deserves
e.g. prosody like

turn for this reason
one found finds requires roses to read

who maybe even
who knows or
who when not only when but who

though even the most one finds indefinitely
paying the vague price
sometimes e.g.

but there is however space
two lines to be shortly possible
that [I] [he] approaches

           ★

a willing suspension of apples
bobbing like friars in the grass
what's the score
why always steel blue eyes to love
does it hurt anymore to slice
little women from the disbelief
of yet another pose of roses

           ★

a medium
a sentimentality
of beginning out of time
out of place
forgetting how to seem
in the wide open spaces of
[nostalgia] [willfulness] [surprise]
pick one
you'll never be another you

           ★

in the face of memory
as if something was to spit out
how unskillfully or fully enough
the record followed to the last dot
she says jubilant that she says
that he says that I say that
after all language is after all
is said and all the camels have
squeaked through the eye of your rose

★

here I sit brokenhearted
fruitless on a throne of air
to jar your cloudiness
or my banality
your partridge in a pear
my plum in the waiting for you
or is it o you beautiful doll
you great big beautiful
or is it

★

turn for any reason not pages
but the sentiment of paper
remember it like a rose
inches from the hopelessly perfect
of one voice you'll wake
and forget to just
picking sighs off the pillowcase
because yes we've got no bananas
we've got none because today

11 *Even*

about to say 'dreams'
[he] [one] [I] dreams
a hand in the bush
pretends 12 in a bell
she paraphrases him
who prefers the atrocity of
begging your pardon
some day I that is I mean
from a military perspective
anything's preferable
even the occupation of dreams

[   ]

was just writing a no matter which
all of none fits
what he never expects to be written
and then again he
thought to sit through
say out the night
up writing is what he pretends
turns on him
the floor turning
the table corners hid in the corners
of his dismembering
what he never expects to be

Alas

false dawn and thunder grown falser
than a glass of spilt milk
a cage a reunion
composed of first lines
where to go from hearing
maybe back to bed or
out the trees through the window
light drip leaves and windshields
gray along the door
ripping muslin bleeding glass
with the bright whisper of a hand

6 *for L. A.*

occasionally without that fatal word

chop chop all too sweetly *-a, -um*

declining the stain the scandal of innocence

of which slide the bread's buttered on or else

or not or else which grieves only the question of

to whom and for how long before even the hillsides the oak

are deciphered infamously in place

The Man Upstairs

doesn't whistle in the shower
desires a little of this and a little of that
wonders whether to shove a flashlight up his ass
unless the act be read symbolic
regrets the existence of alphabets
especially the letter T
though a whisper of dashes tucks us all in
blankets up to our chins
cough moist on the pillow
the siren's falsetto celebrating what's left of a rosebud
the man upstairs pressed so gentle
between the pages of a telephone book

Beyond the
« *End of the Game* »

A Designer's Addendum: one hates to leave too
many blank pages in a book. So I add a small
conclusion adapted from *Amphichroia,* a two-color
assemblage published by The Fault Press. Next
spread, upper left (& then clockwise): Adriano
Spatola, Giulia Niccolai & Paul Vangelisti (the
latter in red) . . .

9 **½**

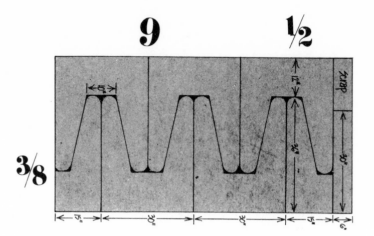

3/8

7

4

POEMA

possibly not now

Paul Vangelisti was born in San Francisco in 1945 and has lived in Los Angeles since 1968 where he continues to work at KPFK (Pacifica). He has published numerous books: *Communion, Air, The Tender Continent, Pearl Harbor, The Extravagant Room,* and *Portfolio;* two works of xerox/collage, *2x2* and *Remembering the Movies;* as well as translations of Adriano Spatola, Giulia Niccolai, Antonio Porta, Vittorio Sereni, Rocco Scotellaro, Franco Beltrametti, Corrado Costa & Mohammed Dib. He edited the experimental audio cassette *Breathing Space 79* (Watershed Foundation, Washington, DC). With John McBride, he edits *Invisible City.*

Designed by John McBride
Composed in Mergenthaler photo-Bembo
by Bill Rock
Printed in the USA